THE DEVIL'S LEFT EAR
AND OTHER MARSHY PLACES

CHARLES R. (BUS) HUMPHREYS

*A PHOTOGRAPHIC GUIDE TO GET INTO
AND OUT OF A SALT MARSH*

THE DEVIL'S LEFT EAR
AND OTHER MARSHY PLACES

CHARLES R. (BUS) HUMPHREYS

THE FIG LEAF PRESS

THE DEVIL'S LEFT EAR
AND OTHER MARSHY PLACES

BY CHARLES R. (BUS) HUMPHREYS

In this part of southeastern North Carolina there are large areas of salt marsh between the barrier islands and the Intracoastal Waterway. Tidal creeks, channels and sloughs form a bewildering maze in these marshes, particularly when viewed at eye level. You can get lost in there. Do not explore this area on a hot summer day on a falling tide. You can get stranded *and* lost. Then Mother Nature turns off the light and the breeze and turns on the sand flies, mosquitos and gnats. They are more voracious than any pride of lions. They will literally eat you alive. If you haven't experienced this, you have never really died! If you survive, the next tide from seven to thirteen hours away will give you enough water to float your boat. Then all you have to do is find your way back out. That's where these aerial photographs come in. It is the reason for this book. I want to be able to find my way out, too.

My first cousin, Priscilla, had a family reunion at Wrightsville Beach, July 20, 1988; people by the barrel and noise to match. Her husband, Grant, an ex-military flier, got his fill of that in a hurry and said to me, "Bus, let's go fly." My answer was, "Great, let me get my camera." He had flown up from Kissimee, Florida, in a two-seater, low-wing monoplane which he has owned and maintained for over thirty years. He understands it and, so help me, I believe it understands him. It was parked at the local Wilmington airport only a short distance away. On the way out he asked, "Any place in particular you want to photograph?" I was more than ready for that one. "Yes, the big marsh between Rich Inlet and Topsail Beach. That's where I do my clamming and oystering and get lost. I'm hoping the pictures will solve that problem."

My contact with the marsh had always been at low altitude, about eye-level, therefore I was not prepared for the scene below as we flew from Rich to Topsail. It was beautiful and startling. The tide was out and the sun was low, a beautiful angle of light, wonderful for photography. The myriad little channels through the spartina were sharply defined, so were the sandbars. An altitude of six hundred feet was just right for a 100mm lense on the Cannon EOS 650. This is an automatic, self-focusing camera. But sometimes, when confronted with water and light reflections, it can't make up its mind and keeps zooming in and out. Also a small plane is not a steady photographic platform. However, shooting at 1/500 of a second helped overcome the jiggle. I took a bunch of pictures, all slides, using ASA 64 Kodachrome film.

When they came back from Eastman I spent several hours studying them carefully to select the ones from which I would have prints made. The twenty-four I chose are included in this book. Locating them with reference to chart no. 11541 of the Intracoastal Waterway, Neuse River to Myrtle Grove Sound (published by U.S. Dept. of Commerce National and Oceanic and Atmospheric Administration, National Ocean Survey), proved to be quite a problem. The chart does not show the marsh area in much detail and even the larger creeks and channels change locations frequently. Sandbars appear and disappear.

Many of the little creeks and channels in the marsh have been named by the watermen who live nearby and earn their living by oystering, clamming, shrimping and fishing. I have known many watermen from the Chesapeake Bay area south, to Pawley's Island, South Carolina. Invariably, they are keen observers of nature. They are intelligent and capable of shrewd conclusions of causes and effects on the activities of the marine life in their area. And they know the minutiae of the geography in that area.

Their skills are diverse. In the past they built many boats and carved most of the decoys used by the gunners. They can repair motors of all kinds and restart a broken motor at sea with nothing but a rusty pair of pliers and a screwdriver. They get home!

They can and do build their own homes. They hang their own nets and they understand the subtle differences between such things as a "set" gill net and a "running" gill net. If a "set" gill net is used in a current it will roll up like a cigar and pick up all the trash on the bottom. If "pin cushions" (sea urchins) are around it will gather them all. You can either throw the net away or spend hours straightening it out and cleaning it. On the other hand, a "running net" is hung in such a way that it does not roll up.

These skills are not taught in school, they are passed down from father to son, generation to generation. New skills are acquired along the way. These watermen have deep roots in their communities extending for many generations. It was from such people I asked help in identifying the channels and creeks in the photographs. I wanted the true names, those given and used by the local people. The two men I asked gave generously of their time and knowledge. Al Sidbury, of Howard Landing near Hampstead, is a waterman who is also engaged in other commercial activities. His family has lived in the area for generations. He loves the water and, when the spot are running, do not expect to find him at home.

He identified the items in the area from Sandy Creek to the "head" of Long Point Channel.

James Perry lives near the Scotts Hill Marina where he grew up. His brother, George, lives down the road two or three blocks where he makes and repairs nets. The Perry family have lived in the area for generations. They both know the marshes intimately.

James pointed out and identified the creeks and channels in that area. It was he, with a twinkle in his eye, who pointed out the "Devil's Left Ear" coming off Green Channel. Witchcraft of ancient days claimed that the devil controlled the left side of the body.

Both men first identified and located the main points of interest in their area on the chart of the Intracoastal Waterway. The modified chart is included in this book following the photographs.

Next, these items were located on the photographs. You will find on each photo small numbers. These locate the features which are identified in the margins below. Most can be cross-referenced to the chart.

If you have a specific destination in mind, study the pictures carefully before you start the trip to locate the best route.

A little more detailed information is required for some of the photos. A creek called Pickin Shoe shows up in photos B & C. I have an idea that when first named, it was "Pick and Choose" as a result of the maze of intersections involved. Over the years "Pick and Choose" degenerated into Pickin Shoe.

Kings Creek is found in photos A, B, & C in back of Topsail Beach. The King Family obviously owned land from near Topsail Beach to Rich Inlet. The name shows up again in photos K, M, N, O, P, Q, R, & T. There is some disagreement among the watermen on the use of "Kings Channel" in photos M & N. Some believe Long Point Channel should be called Kings Channel. Others say Kings Channel is south of Long Point Channel and runs into Kings Mud. Other than that, agreement is remarkably good on other names. The name, Elmore Inlet is used universally. Practically no one refers to it as "Old Topsail Inlet" which is the name on the navigational charts.

In addition to helping me find my way around in the marsh, these photographs also indicate where I should look for clams, oysters, rock crab and fish. When I find a good area, I can locate it on the photo for future reference and I can also return at a later date.

Even a cursory glance at the photos will show why these marshes are such bountiful nursery areas for marine life and our seafood industry.

There are subtle interactions where two inlets are close together. For example, in the Intracoastal Waterway, between Elmore Inlet and Topsail Inlet, there are twice as many "slack water" periods as there are at either inlet. The gill netters take full advantage of these because many fish move in slack water.

These photographs are also of interest because they show the lush, yet stark beauty of what we must consider to be a true wilderness area. That is a difficult concept for those who have long thought of a wilderness as a place of forests, mountains and rushing streams; a place populated by bears, mountain goats and brook trout. But there is as much, if not more, wildlife of great diversity in the marsh.

When raking clams you will sometimes uncover a creature which appears to be a miniature Maine lobster, about an inch long. Its great claw has a trigger device. When set off, the claw closes with great speed. It sounds like a small firecracker. The concussion stuns small minnows on which the creature feeds. This is a "pistol shrimp." There are other equally interesting and unique inhabitants.

The salt marshes are beautiful places indeed, and places of many moods. Some are pure magic. At sun-up in springtime a golden glow falls on the brand new mint-green spartina of the meadows. Then a breeze comes up which adds ribbons of sparks from the channels and creeks. The birds move, some with straight-forward, purposeful flight, others hovering, darting and diving for their breakfast. The skimmers ply the thoroughfares, their mouths open with lower mandible in the water, ever sensitive to the slightest contact with a minnow on which its beak snaps shut. Passing clouds drop their kaleidoscope of shadows.

Later in the day the winds abate and tranquility sets in. This is a time and place of real serenity for mankind, a time of relaxation and release of tensions. Happiness enters the body and diffuses throughout.

The marsh is always changing and no two days are the same. The seasons here in the southland do not change abruptly. They slide from one into the next with only barely perceptible differences. But they change, and life in the marsh follows a definite and age-old pattern. For me, the most beautiful time is the full moon in October. It is enormous as it comes over the sand dunes, dwarfing everything around and covering the misty marsh with an opalescence. It is so beautiful that for some primordial reason you want to cry.

I sincerely hope this booklet will help you find your way about in the marsh and help you understand and enjoy it. And please leave the marsh the way you found it!

PHOTO A

1 Tower on Topsail Beach at Queens Grant Motel
2 Eastern or Banks Channel
3 Intracoastal Waterway
4 Kings Creek
5 Alexander

PHOTO B

1 Crooked Creek
2 Pickin Shoe Creek
3 Kings Creek
4 Goat Hammock (Howard Family)
5 Tower on Topsail Beach

PHOTO C

1 Kings Creek
2 Pickin Shoe Creek
3 Old House Creek

PHOTO D

1 Topsail Channel
2 Old House Creek
3 Eastern or Banks Channel
4 Topsail Beach

PHOTO E

1 Topsail Inlet
2 Old House Creek
3 Topsail Channel
4 Black Mud Channel
5 Howard Channel
6 (There is no name for this creek)

PHOTO F

1 Topsail Beach
2 Banks Channel
3 Topsail Channel
4 Old House Creek

PHOTO G

1 Topsail Inlet
2 Black Mud Channel
3 Howard Channel
4 Big Creek
5 Banks Channel

PHOTO H

1 Topsail Inlet
2 Howard Channel
3 Big Creek
4 Middle Creek
5 Little Creek
6 Lea Island

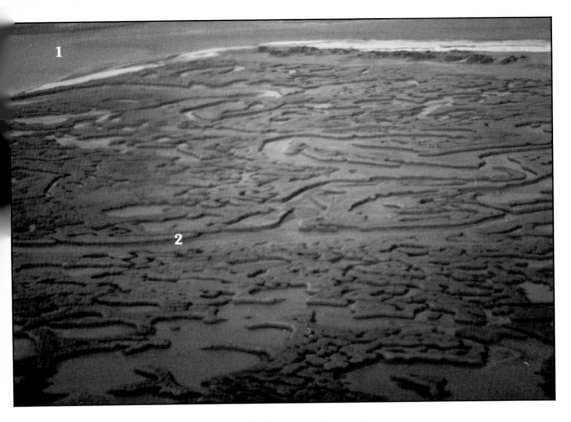

PHOTO I   **1** Topsail Channel
           2 Buck Creek (Topsail to Howard Channel)

PHOTO J

1 Buck Creek
2 Topsail Channel
3 Old House Creek

PHOTO K

1 Topsail Inlet
2 Houses on Lea Island
3 Little Pittman
4 Pittman
5 Long Point Channel or "Kings Channel"

PHOTO L

1 Lea Island
2 Howard Channel
3 Little Pittman
4 Pittman

PHOTO O

1 Elmore Inlet
2 Lea Island
3 Long Point Channel or "Kings Channel"
4 Pittman
5 "Kings Channel"

PHOTO P

1 Elmore Inlet
2 Head
3 "Kings Channel"
4 Hutaff Island

PHOTO Q

1 Elmore Inlet
2 Hutaff Island
3 "Kings Channel"
4 Intracoastal Waterway
5 Long Point Channel or "Kings Channel"

PHOTO R

1 Elmore Inlet
2 Head
3 King's Mud
4 Hammock Island
5 Pin Cushion Creek
6 Stone Crab Creek
7 Hammock Creek

PHOTO S

1 Hutaff Island
2 Green Channel
3 Hammock Creek
4 Pin Cushion Creek
5 Stone Crab Creek
6 Devil's Left Ear

PHOTO T

1 Hutaff Island
2 "Kings Channel"
3 Head
4 Kings Mud

PHOTO U

1 Hutaff Island
2 Green Channel
3 Deep Creek
4 House & Dock

PHOTO V

1 Green Channel
2 House & Dock
3 Half-a-Bushel Creek

PHOTO W

1 Hutaff Island
2 House & Dock
3 Rich Inlet
4 Green Channel

PHOTO X

1 Rich Inlet
2 Figure 8 Island
3 Figure 8 Island Creek
4 Nixon Channel

PHOTO M

1 Elmore Inlet
2 Lea Island
3 Little Pittman
4 Pittman
5 Long Point Channel or "Kings Channel"

PHOTO N

1 Elmore Inlet
2 Long Point Channel or "Kings Channel"
3 Intracoastal Waterway
4 Lea Island